JESUS

JESUS is LORD

Visit the author's website:

www.jesusislord.org.uk

PREFACE

Blessing of the LORD

"The LORD bless you and keep you;

The LORD make His face shine on you,

And be gracious to you;

The LORD lift up His countenance upon you,

And give you peace."

in LORD JESUS CHRIST Name,

amen and amen.

JESUS is LORD

DEDICATION

I would like to dedicate this book to my LORD Jesus Christ the GOD Almighty who was, and is, and is to come, amen and amen.

JESUS is LORD

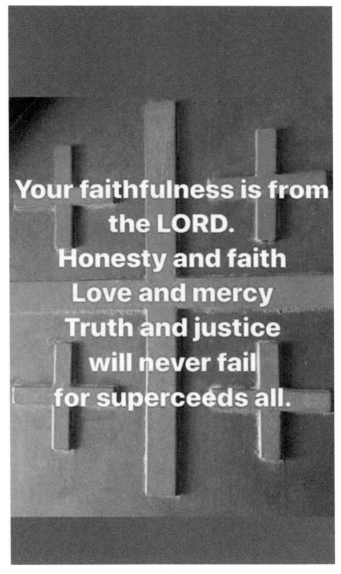

Your faithfulness is from
the LORD.
Honesty and faith
Love and mercy
Truth and justice
will never fail
for superceeds all.

1

You will be vindicated in Me for it is the heritage of the servants of the LORD!

Command all unclean spirits to come out of people's life. Command for them to leave in My name. Freely freely you have received freely freely you give.

Rise up, be strong. My hand is not short that cannot save. Rise up before Me for all eyes to see, you are blessed of the LORD.

The battle is the LORD's
the victory is yours!
The sound of the beating drums
filling the atmosphere
announcing
LORD's vindication of you.
Get up O you servant
the LORD is here!
He came with many gifts.
He clothed you in
righteousness, glory and honor.
The victory
has already been won!

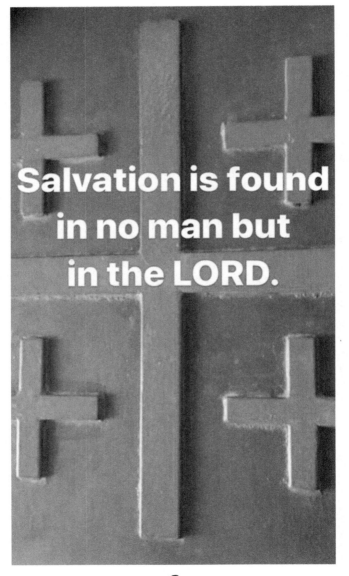

6

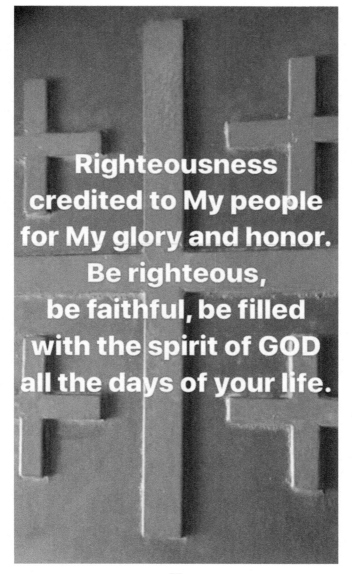

Righteousness
credited to My people
for My glory and honor.
Be righteous,
be faithful, be filled
with the spirit of GOD
all the days of your life.

Harvest is plentiful, the workers are a few. Do your works in Me. I have gifted from high above, I have awarded you the crown of righteousness for you to live for My glory and honour.

The doors of My Kingdom open for all whoever believes in Me, will live through Me.

I, Myself brought you out of Egypt gave you this land. Live in the land peacefully.
Do not despise anyone or anything.
I am your shield I will protect you.

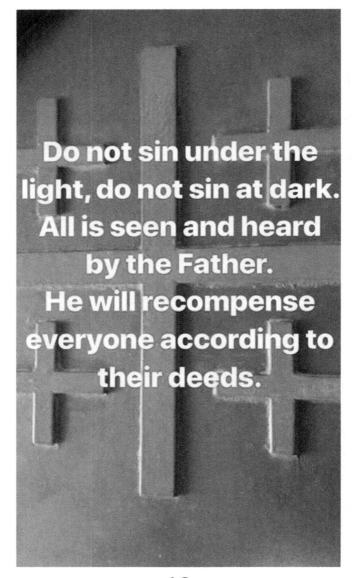

Do not sin under the light, do not sin at dark. All is seen and heard by the Father. He will recompense everyone according to their deeds.

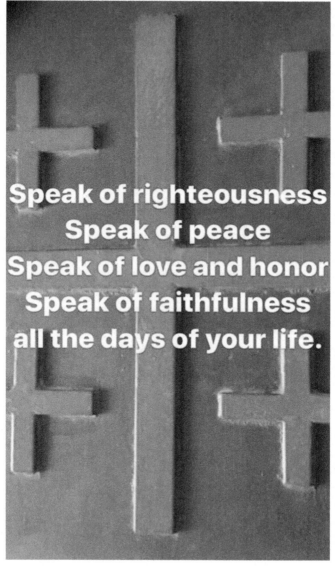

13

14

Do not fear
for I am with you
I will guide you every
step of the way into
your destiny.
You are with me
in this age and in the
new!

You will hear from Me
one way or other.
My instructions are
sealed in you.
Obey My will.
Choose to live in Me
with Me through Me.

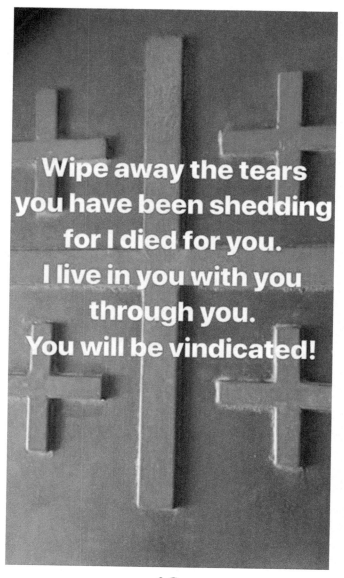

18

Those who persecuted
My prophets whom I sent
all your wrong doings will
be repaid with
double destruction.
Whoever wants to be first
among you will be last
and whoever is the least
among you will be made
first.

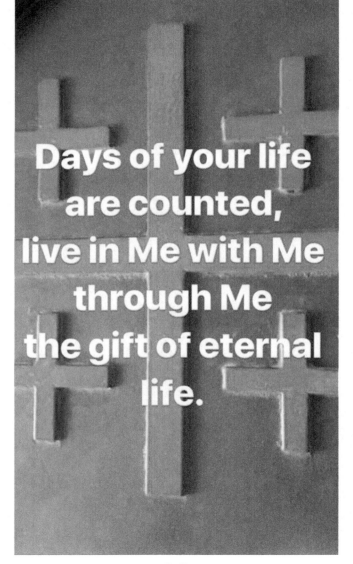

My kingdom is yours
now and forever.
You are raised in
Christ
You are knitted in
love
You are embedded in
Me for an eternal life!

Faith of a servant moves mountain for their trust is in Me.

www.ministryofchristuk.co.uk

24

You have been raised in Christ for eternal life.
You are the chosen nation for the LORD to live in Him.
Accept your calling.

25

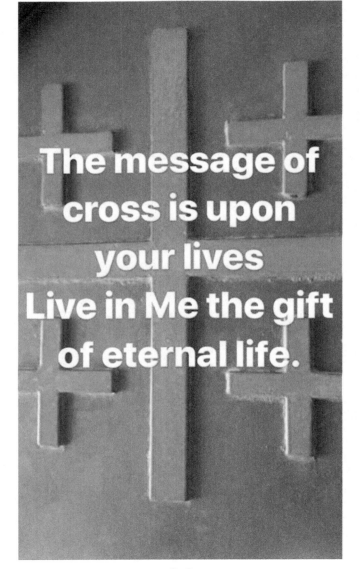

The message of
cross is upon
your lives
Live in Me the gift
of eternal life.

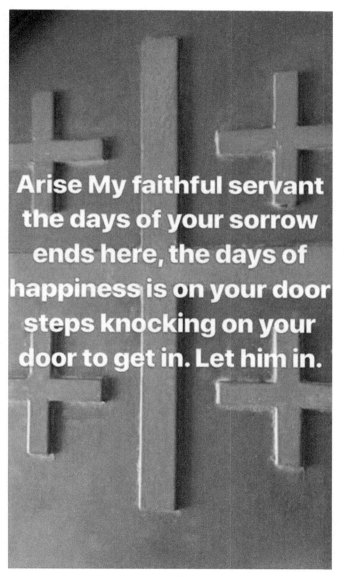

Arise My faithful servant the days of your sorrow ends here, the days of happiness is on your door steps knocking on your door to get in. Let him in.

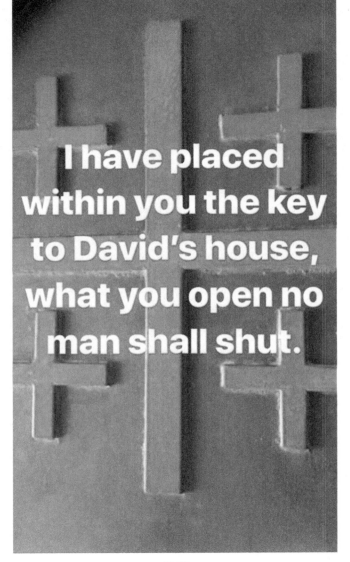

I have placed within you the key to David's house, what you open no man shall shut.

All that is asked you
will be given
All that is promised to
you you will receive.
Behold, My hand is
not shortened that
it cannot save!

Rewards are given out to
faithful servant
at due time.
You have been rewarded
for all your hard works
you put into
for the salvation of
mankind.

The days of sorrow and
sadness will disappear.
You are the child of
GOD who live in Me.
Stand up strong.
The richness of My
glory upon you.
You are rich in Christ.

Gift of GOD is eternal life given in LORD Jesus Christ whoever believes in Him shall not perish but have an eternal life.

Your prayers are heard in heavens.
Pray for My people, pray for each and everyone of them to have My Kingdom in their life for their salvation upon their life.

34

The word that I have spoken is to establish you, not to tear you. The LORD your GOD has spoken will He not do it? I gave My promise to you will I not perform it? My Word is life, I am the giver of life.

The beautifulness of the soul flows in you through you.
You are surrounded by holy angels, the uplifting arm of the LORD is upon you.
Live in peace.

You are seated in
the heavenly places
in Christ Jesus.
Be strong,
have courage
for I have overcome
the world.

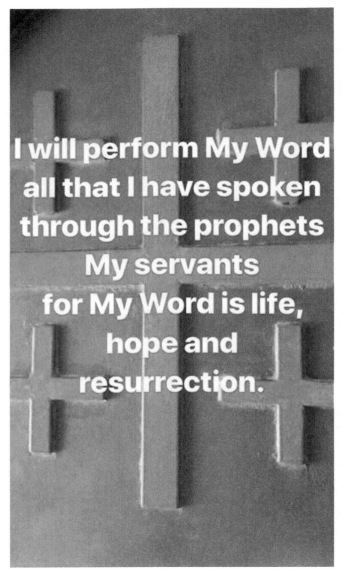

I will perform My Word
all that I have spoken
through the prophets
My servants
for My Word is life,
hope and
resurrection.

Guard your heart
everything you do
flows from it.
Keep your heart pure,
your lips clean
for you are holy to the
LORD.

Today many of the first day.
Today I give you My Kingdom
at your door step.
Rise up above all.
Seek the Kingdom of GOD
and justice
for what they have done
to you will be undone.

Have faith.
I will do what I say
I will bring My
Kingdom on earth.
I will raise up children
of GOD on the
last day.

41

42

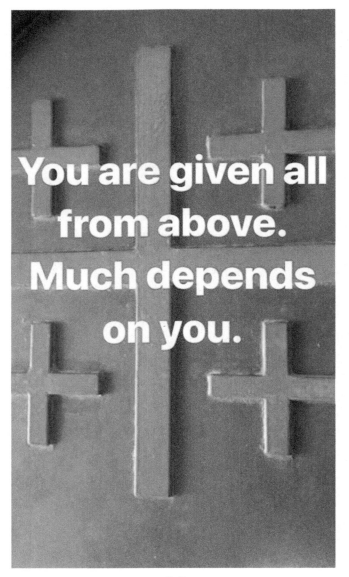

44

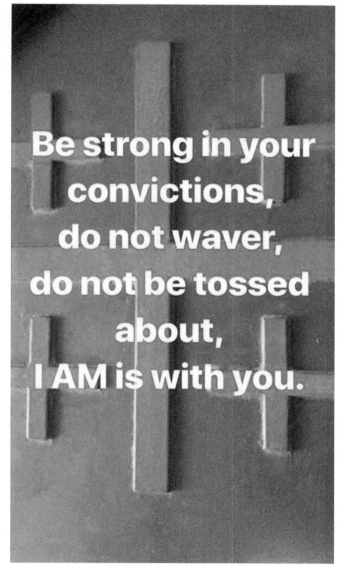

Be strong in your convictions,
do not waver,
do not be tossed about,
I AM is with you.

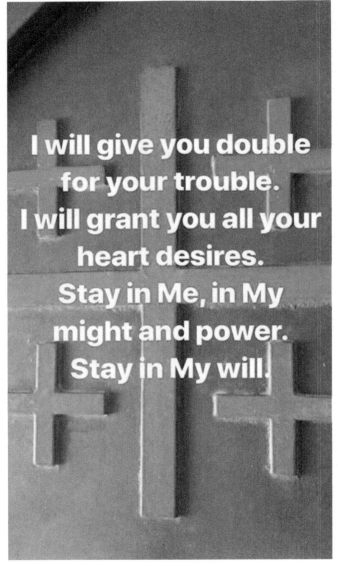

I will give you double
for your trouble.
I will grant you all your
heart desires.
Stay in Me, in My
might and power.
Stay in My will.

Do not sin.
Do not sin against heaven
and against anyone.
Do not bring charges
against your brothers and
sisters who are in Christ!
All created for My glory
and honour!

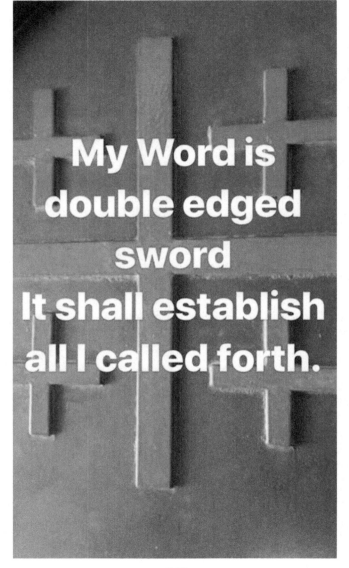

48

Walk with Me in My statutes and commandments. They are given for your good so that you do not sin.

Praise the LORD,
all you nations!
LORD has a will for
your life it shall
surely be!
LORD has spoken it
shall come to pass!

The Kingdom of God does not come with observation, nor it is here and there. By your righteousness possessed in your soul.

Have peace and joy
in your heart.
Peace of GOD
surpasses all
understanding,
put your trust in Me.

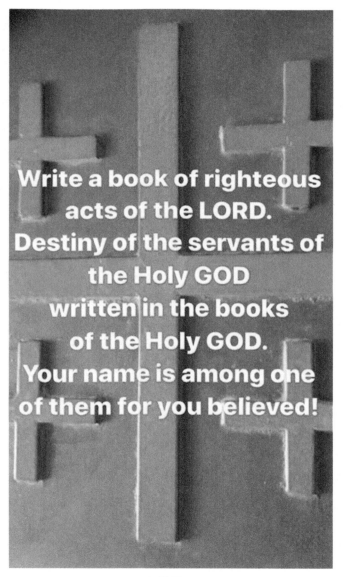

Write a book of righteous
acts of the LORD.
Destiny of the servants of
the Holy GOD
written in the books
of the Holy GOD.
Your name is among one
of them for you believed!

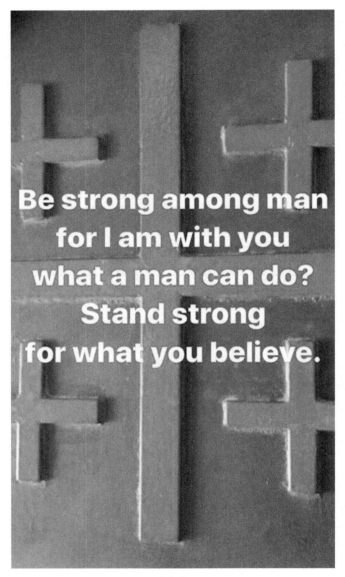

Be strong among man
for I am with you
what a man can do?
Stand strong
for what you believe.

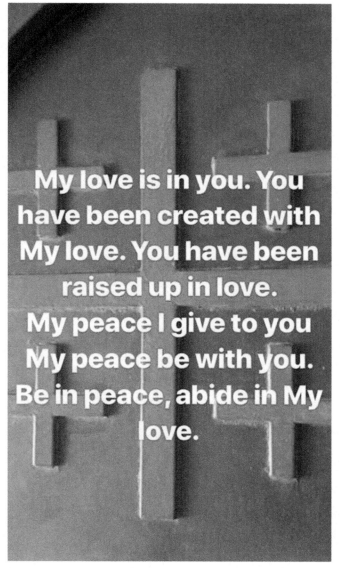

My love is in you. You have been created with My love. You have been raised up in love.
My peace I give to you My peace be with you. Be in peace, abide in My love.

Truly I say to you
unless you forgive others
you won't be forgiven.
Forgiveness
is prerequisite in
the Kingdom of GOD
Forgive all.

Have no fear of the wicked and their schemes against you for no arrows of the wicked will prevail against you for I am your shield.

The choices
you make in life
determines
who you are with
in the eternity.
Choose right.

The day is not over yet, the night has not come yet, while you still have the opportunity repent of all your sins. Repentance is prerequisite for the life of obedience in Me!

59

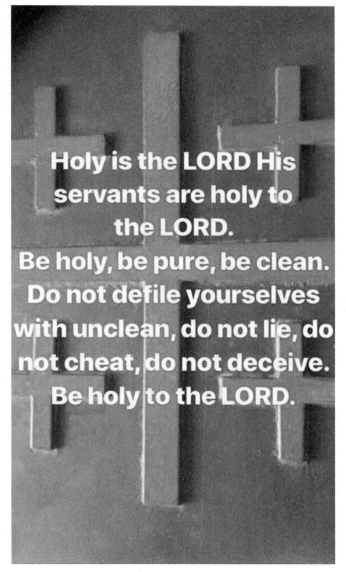

Holy is the LORD His servants are holy to the LORD.
Be holy, be pure, be clean.
Do not defile yourselves with unclean, do not lie, do not cheat, do not deceive.
Be holy to the LORD.

You will receive all My promises to you for you believed.

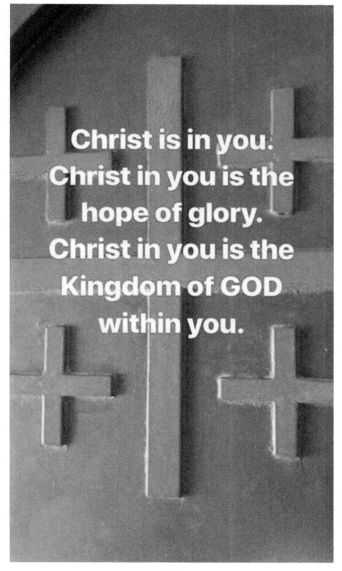

Christ is in you.
Christ in you is the
hope of glory.
Christ in you is the
Kingdom of GOD
within you.

I invite each and everyone one of you to pray with me for our sisters and brothers who lost their lives in Sri Lanka this morning for their belief in the LORD.

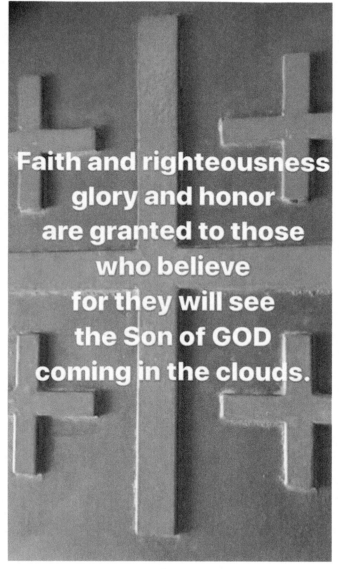

Faith and righteousness
glory and honor
are granted to those
who believe
for they will see
the Son of GOD
coming in the clouds.

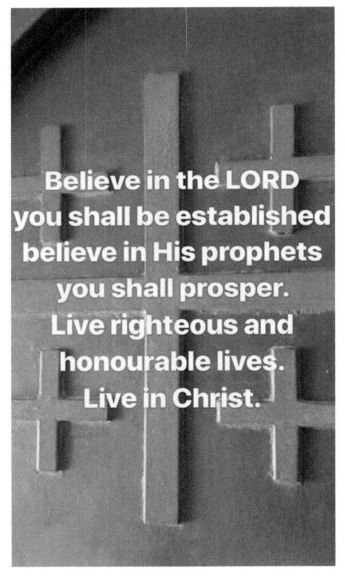

Believe in the LORD
you shall be established
believe in His prophets
you shall prosper.
Live righteous and
honourable lives.
Live in Christ.

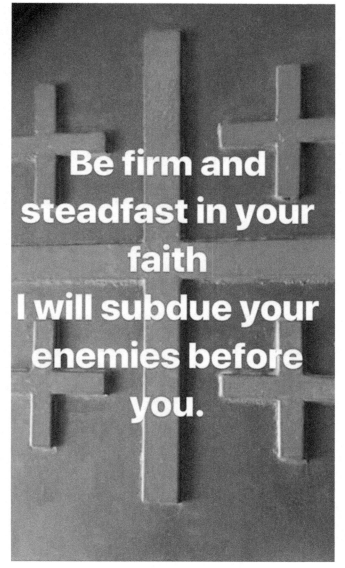

67

Time is running out,
for all to come to
repentance is
prerequisite
for eternal life
given in Me.

You have My power in you within you. My power is made perfect in your weakness. Arise! Stand up strong in the face of opposition. Do not fear for I am with you.

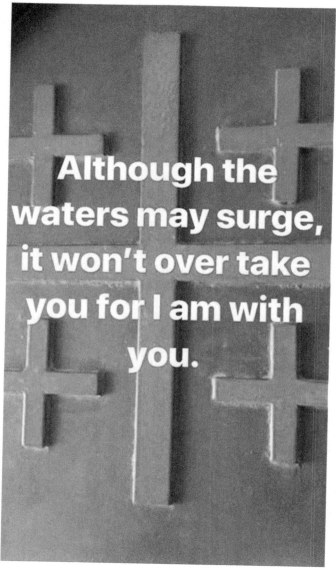

Although the waters may surge, it won't over take you for I am with you.

71

It is written My children do not sin for they live in Me. They repent, they wash their inequities in My blood, they live in Me.

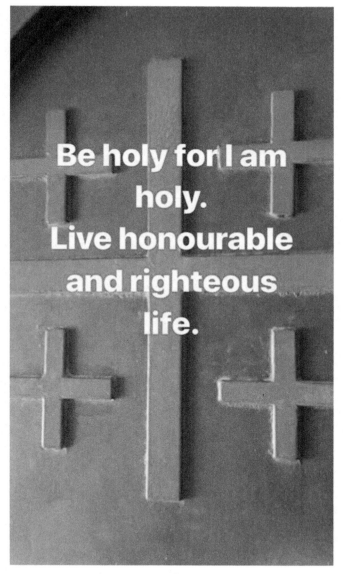

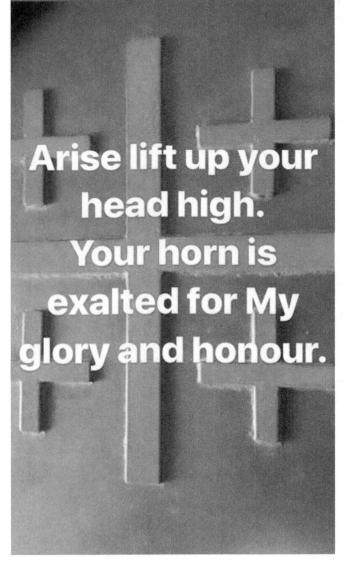

74

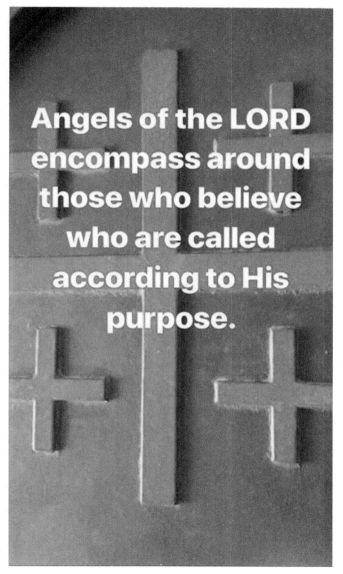

Angels of the LORD encompass around those who believe who are called according to His purpose.

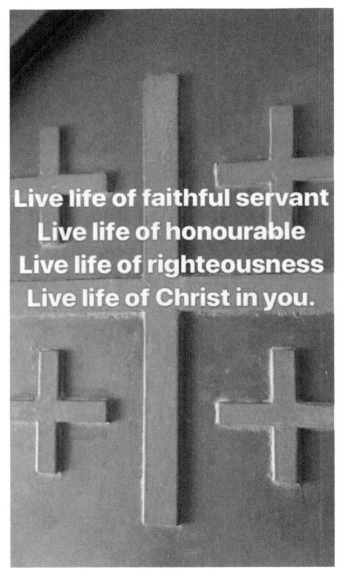

Live life of faithful servant
Live life of honourable
Live life of righteousness
Live life of Christ in you.

Only I and I can make it
happen for you, only I
and I can open the
closed doors for you,
only I can bring the
salvation upon you.
Your salvation is in Me.
Come to Me!

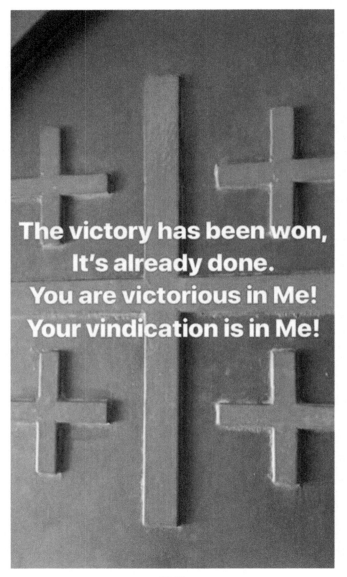

78

Be joyful and
fruitful
Be happy and
peaceful
Be wondrous and
faithful
in the LORD.

You will find the right way
You will find My way
You will bring
My Kingdom to earth
for I am with you
who can be against you.

82

The Kingdom of GOD at
work in you
within you you will find
peace, within you is the
salvation of GOD,
within you is the Kingdom
of GOD and it's riches
within you is
the Son of GOD!

You have been created
with love.
Love is in you.
Love is above all for
GOD is Love.
GOD so loved the world
He gave His one and
only Son.
Love all.

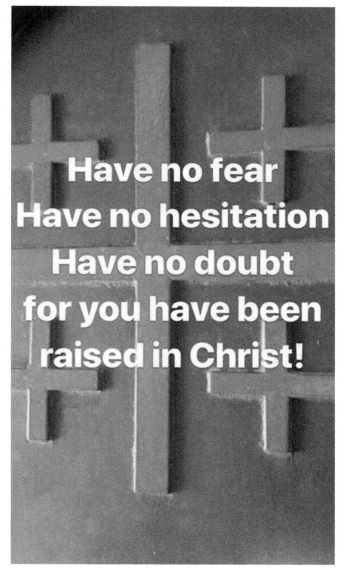

Live life of a faithful and
the truth,
in you is the Son of GOD
with you is His Holy Spirit
through you is the
Kingdom of GOD
and it's righteousness.

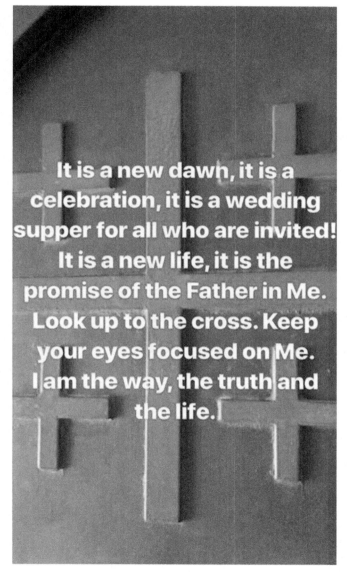

It is a new dawn, it is a celebration, it is a wedding supper for all who are invited! It is a new life, it is the promise of the Father in Me. Look up to the cross. Keep your eyes focused on Me. I am the way, the truth and the life.

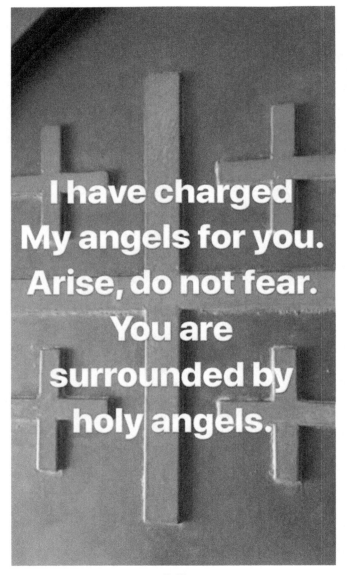

I have charged
My angels for you.
Arise, do not fear.
You are
surrounded by
holy angels.

The end result is
guaranteed,
you are triumphant
in Me!
Therefore
be confident, be bold,
be courageous
in all your works.

Wipe away the tears you have been shedding. Stay strong Your vindication is near.

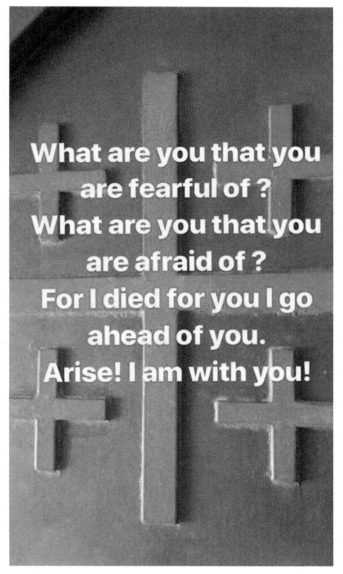

91

Come in humility.
Humble yourselves
before Me.
Come in before Me
for perfect love.

Rejoice in Me!
Under any circumstances that
you face rejoice always, bring
joy to My people.
Be joyful!
Your very rewards are in Me.
I say rejoice!

You are the apple of
My eye. You are the
rising sun shine.
Live for Me.
Shine your light
before Me.

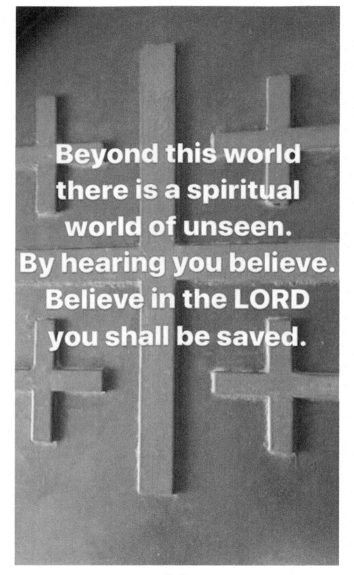

Beyond this world
there is a spiritual
world of unseen.
By hearing you believe.
Believe in the LORD
you shall be saved.

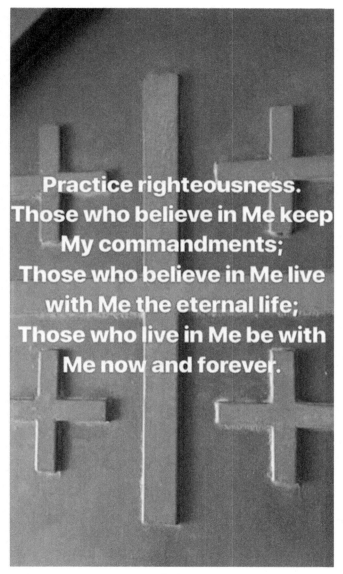

Practice righteousness.
Those who believe in Me keep
My commandments;
Those who believe in Me live
with Me the eternal life;
Those who live in Me be with
Me now and forever.

100

JESUS is LORD

May the grace of the Lord Jesus Christ, and the love of God, and the fellowship of the Holy Spirit be with you all.

2 Corinthians 13:14

Printed in Great Britain
by Amazon